GROOVY
GEOMETRY

Also in the Magical Math series

Dazzling Division

Delightful Decimals and Perfect Percents

Fabulous Fractions

Marvelous Multiplication

Measurement Mania

Magical Math

GROOVY GEOMETRY

Games and Activities
That Make Math Easy and Fun

Lynette Long

JOSSEY-BASS
A Wiley Imprint
www.josseybass.com

Published by Jossey-Bass
A Wiley Imprint
989 Market Street, San Francisco, CA 94103-1741   www.josseybass.com

Illustrations copyright © 2003 by Tina Cash-Walsh

Published simultaneously in Canada

Jossey-Bass books and products are available through most bookstores. To contact Jossey-Bass directly call our Customer Care Department within the U.S. at 800-956-7739, outside the U.S. at 317-572-3986, or fax 317-572-4002.

Jossey-Bass also publishes its books in a variety of electronic formats. Some content that appears in print may not be available in electronic books.

Library of Congress Cataloging-in-Publication Data

Long, Lynette.
    Groovy geometry : games and activities that make math easy and fun / Lynette Long.
       p. cm.
    Includes index.
     ISBN 0-471-21059-5 (pbk. : alk. paper)
      1. Geometry—Study and teaching (Elementary)—Activity programs. 2. Games in mathematics education. I. Title.

QA462.2.G34 L36 2003
372.7—dc21   2002068996

Printed in the United States of America
FIRST EDITION
PB Printing   10 9 8 7 6 5 4

Contents

I. The Magic of Geometry — 1

II. Angles — 3

1 Measure Up — 5
2 Draw It! — 8
3 Name Game — 11
4 Angle Pairs — 13
5 Color by Angles — 15
6 Perpendicular Numbers — 18
7 Right-Angle Scavenger Hunt — 20

III. Triangles — 23

8 Triangle Collage — 25
9 Triangle Memory — 27
10 Triangle Angles — 29
11 Outside the Triangle — 31
12 Triangle Area — 35
13 Two the Same — 39
14 How Tall? — 42
15 Perfect Squares — 45
16 Pythagorean Proof — 49

IV. Quadrilaterals — 53

17 Crazy about Quadrilaterals — 55
18 Quadrilateral Angles — 58
19 String Shapes — 61
20 Doubt It! — 62
21 Rectangle Race — 64

22 Parallelogram Presto Change-O   66

23 Pattern Blocks   68

24 Shape Storybook   71

V. Circles   73

25 Around and Around   75

26 Finding Pi   77

27 Bicycle Odometer   80

28 Circle Area   81

29 Pizza Party   83

30 Central Angles   86

VI. Solids   89

31 Solid Shapes   91

32 Cereal Surfaces   94

33 Cylinder Surfaces   95

34 Cube Construction   97

35 Volume of a Cylinder   99

36 Building Blocks   101

VII. Odds and Ends   103

37 Shape Comparison   105

38 Bull's Eye   107

39 Mystery Picture   110

40 Number Symmetry   112

Geometry Master Certificate   115

Index   117

THE MAGIC OF GEOMETRY

Geometry is the study of points, lines, angles, and shapes, and their relationships and properties. It sounds like a lot to know, but much of it is already in your head. Geometry is all around us. If people didn't think about geometry, they wouldn't be able to build great structures such as the pyramids, or even simple things that lie flat such as a table.

Geometry can be easily learned by experimenting and having fun with things you can find around the house. You can learn most of the principles of geometry using cereal boxes, soda cans, plates, string, magazines, and other common household objects. So get ready to have a great time exploring the world of geometry.

SOME KEY TERMS TO KNOW

Geometry starts with the concepts of lines, points, rays, and planes. You probably already have a pretty good idea of what lines and points are, but in geometry these terms have a more specific meaning than in everyday life. Here are some words and definitions you'll need to know:

Plane: a flat surface that extends infinitely in all directions

Point: a location on a plane

Line: a straight path of points that goes on indefinitely

Line segment: all of the points on a line between two specific end points

Ray: all of the points on a line going out from one end point indefinitely in one direction

Plane geometry: the study of two-dimensional figures

Solid geometry: the study of three-dimensional figures

II

ANGLES

An **angle** is formed by the meeting of two rays at the same end point. The point where the two rays meet is called the angle's **vertex.** The rays are called the sides of the angle.

Angles are everywhere. When you bend your arm, your elbow becomes the vertex of the angle formed by the two parts of your arm. When two streets cross each other, they form angles. Here are some examples of angles:

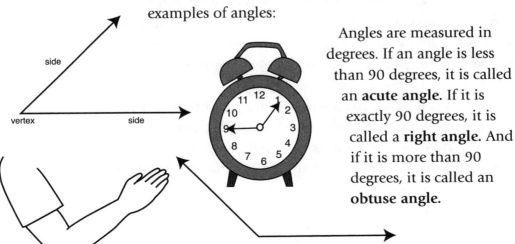

Angles are measured in degrees. If an angle is less than 90 degrees, it is called an **acute angle.** If it is exactly 90 degrees, it is called a **right angle.** And if it is more than 90 degrees, it is called an **obtuse angle.**

3

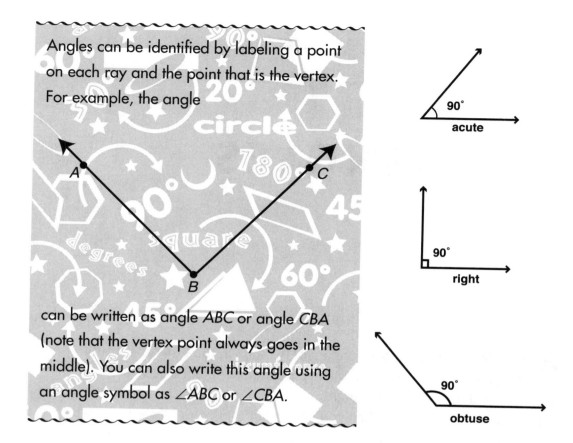

Angles can be identified by labeling a point on each ray and the point that is the vertex. For example, the angle

can be written as angle *ABC* or angle *CBA* (note that the vertex point always goes in the middle). You can also write this angle using an angle symbol as ∠*ABC* or ∠*CBA*.

90°
acute

90°
right

90°
obtuse

In this section, you'll practice measuring and creating different angles, learn the relationship between some interesting angle pairs, discover the relationship between the angles formed when two parallel lines are intersected by another line, practice recognizing right angles and perpendicular lines, and more.

Along the way, you'll measure angles around your house, have an angle-drawing competition, play a game of matching angle pairs, create numbers using only perpendicular lines, and go on a right-angle scavenger hunt. These activities will teach you more than you can imagine about angles, so why not get started?

Measure Up

Angles are measured in degrees using a **protractor**.
If you've never used one, don't worry. It's easy and fun.
You just align the bottom marking of the protractor with one
ray of the angle you want to measure. The vertex of the angle
should be seen through the hole in the protractor. Next, read
the number on the protractor nearest to where the second ray
crosses. Your protractor has two sets of numbers. The one you
use depends on the starting direction of the angle. You need to
figure out which set of numbers has the first ray starting at
zero, then count up from there to find the right number. Try
this activity to practice measuring angles with a protractor.

MATERIALS

protractor
pencil
paper
scissors
cardboard
ruler
paper brad

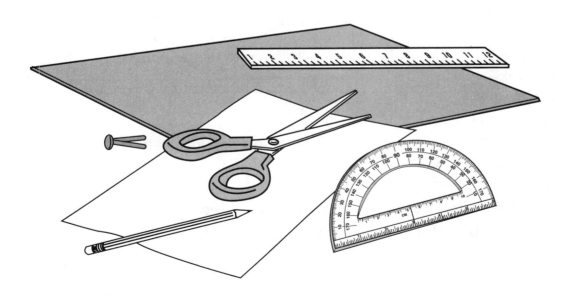

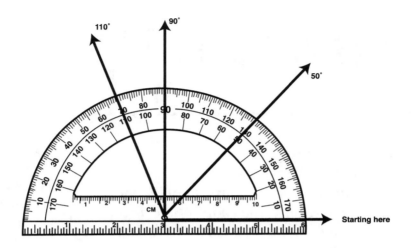

Procedure

1. Look around any room in your house for lines that meet at corners—for example, tables, picture frames, blocks, books, clock hands, and so on.

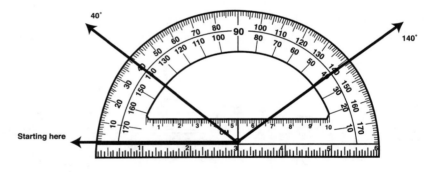

Measuring angles with a protractor

2. Use the protractor to measure some of the angles created by the things in the room.

3. Write down the name of the thing and the angle on a piece of paper.

4. When you've measured at least six things, look at your list of measurements. What is the most common angle measurement on your list?

5. Cut out two strips from the cardboard that are about 1 inch (2.5 cm) × 8 inches (20 cm). Use a ruler to draw a ray down the middle of each strip. Connect the strips of cardboard at the end points of the two rays using the paper brad.

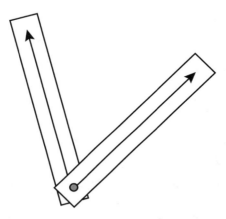

6. Use the cardboard rays to make different angles and measure the angles with your protractor.

Draw It!

Try this game to practice drawing angles of different measures.

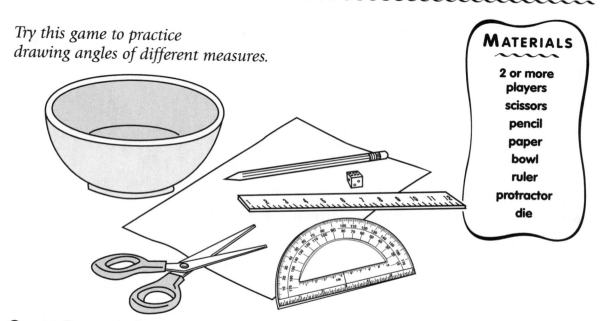

Game Preparation

1. Cut each sheet of paper into eight small pieces.

2. Write one of the following measurements on each small piece of paper:

10 degrees	50 degrees	135 degrees
15 degrees	65 degrees	145 degrees
20 degrees	75 degrees	160 degrees
30 degrees	90 degrees	170 degrees
40 degrees	100 degrees	
45 degrees	120 degrees	

3. Fold the pieces of paper so that you can't see the measurements and place them in the bowl.

Game Rules

1. Player 1 reaches into the bowl and picks a piece of paper. Player 1 reads the number of degrees out loud and tries to draw an angle with this measure using only a pencil and a ruler.

2. Player 2, using a protractor, measures the angle drawn and writes the measure of the angle inside the angle.

3. Player 2 finds the difference between the measure of the angle as noted on the paper and the actual measure of the angle drawn.

4. Player 1 rolls a single die. If the difference between the measure of the angle drawn and the measure on the piece of paper is less than the number rolled, then Player 1 earns 1 point.

> **EXAMPLE** ~~~~~~
> Player 1 is supposed to draw a 30-degree angle, but when Player 2 measures it using a protractor, the angle is actually 34 degrees. The difference between these two measures is 4 degrees (34 − 30 = 4). Player 1 rolls a 5 on the die. Player 1 earns 1 point, since the difference of 4 degrees is less than the number rolled, which is 5.

5. Player 2 selects a piece of paper from the bowl, reads the number of degrees out loud, and tries to draw an angle with that measure. Player 1 measures the angle drawn with a protractor and writes the measure. Player 2 rolls the die to determine if his or her drawing is accurate enough to earn a point.

6. The first player to earn 3 points wins the game.

BRAIN Stretcher

Create new slips of paper and write new angle measures on them. Make the angles measure between 0 and 360 degrees. Play the game again using these new measures.

Name Game

Play this fast-paced game to practice identifying acute, right, and obtuse angles (see pages 3–4 for definitions and examples).

MATERIALS

2 players
pencil
16 index cards

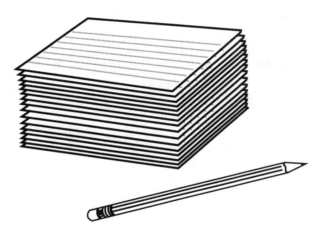

Game Preparation

Write one of the following degree measurements on each of the index cards:

10 degrees	70 degrees	130 degrees
20 degrees	80 degrees	140 degrees
30 degrees	90 degrees	150 degrees
40 degrees	100 degrees	160 degrees
50 degrees	110 degrees	
60 degrees	120 degrees	

Game Rules

1. Deal eight cards to each player.

2. Both players put their cards facedown in a stack in front of them.

3. Players turn over their top cards at the same time and put them down faceup next to each other.

4. Each player calls out at the same time whether his or her angle is acute, right, or obtuse. An obtuse angle beats a right or an acute angle, and a right angle beats an acute angle. The winner gets to keep both cards. If the angles are both acute or both obtuse, then the largest angle wins. If the angles are both right, then the winner of the next round gets to keep the cards. If a player calls out the wrong type of angle, then he or she loses the round no matter what angle is showing on the card.

5. When all the cards have been played, the player with the most cards is the winner.

Angle Pairs

Angles also have different names that refer to special relation-ships that some angles have with other angles. These pairs of angles are called vertical, complementary, and supplementary. **Vertical angles** *are opposite angles that are formed when two lines intersect. They have the same measurement. For exam-ple, if the original angle is 31 degrees, the vertical angle is 31 degrees.* **Complementary angles** *are angles whose measurements add up to 90 degrees. For example, if the original angle is 12 degrees, the complementary angle meas-ures 78 degrees (90 − 12 = 78).* **Sup-plementary angles** *are angles whose measurements add up to 180 degrees. For example, if the original angle is 25 degrees, the sup-plementary angle measures 155 degrees (180 − 25 = 155). Play this game to practice computing the measures of complementary, supplementary, and vertical angles.*

MATERIALS

2 players
pencil
15 index cards
dice

Game Preparation

1. Write the words *vertical angles* on five index cards. Write the words *comple-mentary angles* on five index cards. Write the words *supplementary angles* on five index cards.

Game Rules

1. Shuffle the cards and deal each player seven cards. There should be one card left over. Place this card facedown in the center of the table.

2. Player 1 rolls the dice and uses the numbers rolled to form a two-digit number. The larger number rolled is the tens place and the smaller number rolled is the ones place. For example, if a 6 and a 4 are rolled, the number rolled is 64. This is the number of your original angle.

3. Players each select one of their index cards and place it faceup on the table. If the cards are the same, Player 2 turns over another card until he or she gets a different type of angle card.

4. Players compute the value of the type of angle named on their cards from the original angle. The player with the larger angle wins both cards.

EXAMPLE ~~~~~~

The number rolled is 55. Player 1 selected a vertical angle card. The vertical angle of an angle that measures 55 degrees is an angle that measures 55 degrees. Player 2 selected a complementary angle card. The complementary angle of an angle that measures 55 degrees is 35 degrees (90 − 55 = 35). Player 1 wins both cards, since 55 degrees is greater than 35 degrees.

5. Players take turns rolling the dice and calculating the angles until the cards have run out. The winner is the player with the most cards at the end of the game.

5

Color by Angles

Parallel lines are lines on the same plane that will never intersect. A **transversal** is a line that intersects two parallel lines. When two parallel lines are cut by a transversal, they form eight angles. The angles can be named according to their position.

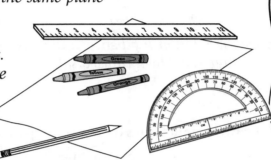

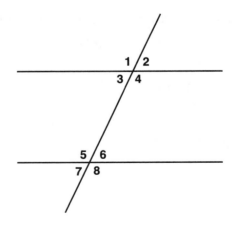

MATERIALS

ruler

pencil

paper

crayons or colored pencils

protractor

Angles between the two parallel lines are **interior angles.**

Angles 3, 4, 5, and 6 are interior angles

Angles outside the parallel lines are **exterior angles.**

Angles 1, 2, 7, and 8 are exterior angles

Angles on opposite sides of the transversal that have the same measurement are **alternate angles.**

Angles 3 and 6 are alternate interior angles

Angles 4 and 5 are alternate interior angles

Parallel lines cut by a transversal

Angles 1 and 8 are alternate exterior angles

Angles 2 and 7 are alternate exterior angles

Angles on the same side of the transversal that have the same measurement are **corresponding angles**.

Angles 1 and 5 are corresponding angles

Angles 2 and 6 are corresponding angles

Angles 3 and 7 are corresponding angles

Angles 4 and 8 are corresponding angles

Try this activity to see the relationship between the angles formed when two parallel lines are intersected by a transversal.

Procedure

1. Using a ruler, draw two parallel lines on a piece of paper.

2. Using a ruler, draw a transversal across the lines.

3. Label the eight angles 1, 2, 3, 4, 5, 6, 7, and 8, as in the illustration on page 15.

4. Using a protractor, measure each of the angles. Write the measures on a separate piece of paper.

Angle 1 =

Angle 2 =

Angle 3 =

Angle 4 =

Angle 5 =

Angle 6 =

Angle 7 =

Angle 8 =

5. Use crayons or colored pencils to color the space inside all the angles with the same measure one color. How many different colors did you use?

6. Add any two angles with different measures. What is the sum of these two angles?

Tips and Tricks

Any two different angles in the figure will be supplementary angles, which means they will always add up to 180 degrees.

BRAIN Stretcher

Find the alternate interior and exterior angles and the corresponding angles in the picture you colored.

circumference

Perpendicular Numbers

A right angle is an angle of 90 degrees. Two lines that meet in a right angle are called **perpendicular lines.** Try this activity to form numbers using only perpendicular lines.

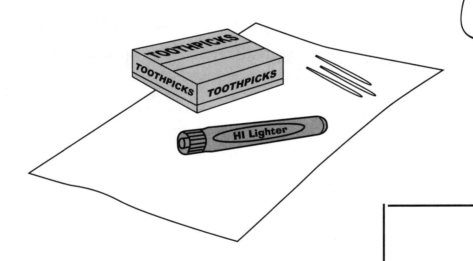

Procedure

1. Using a highlighter, copy the following diagram on a piece a paper. Make each of the line segments as long as one of your toothpicks.

2. Use your toothpicks to cover each of the seven segments. You have made the number 8 using only perpendicular lines.

3. Now see if you can use the toothpicks to make all the numbers from 0 to 9 using only perpendicular lines. (Hint: use the highlighted lines from the number 8 figure as a base from which to create the rest of the numbers.)

4. How many right angles can you find in each number?

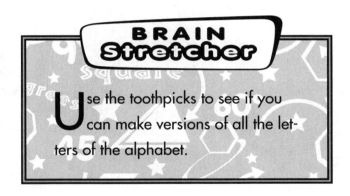

BRAIN Stretcher

Use the toothpicks to see if you can make versions of all the letters of the alphabet.

7 Right-Angle Scavenger Hunt

*Now that you know what right angles look
like, play this game to discover the right
angles in a home.*

MATERIALS

2 or more
players
pencil
index cards
brown paper bag
paper

Game Preparation

1. Using the home of one player, write the name of each room on an index card.

2. Fold the index cards and place them in a brown paper bag.

Game Rules

1. Each player reaches into the bag and selects an index card.

2. Players each have 10 minutes to go into the room they selected and make a list on paper of as many right angles as they can find. (Hint: you can use a corner of your index card as a right-angle tester.)

3. After 10 minutes, players read their lists to each other. The player with the longest list wins the game.

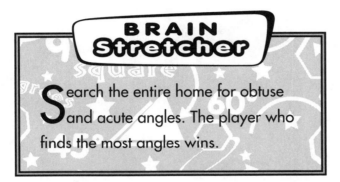

BRAIN Stretcher

Search the entire home for obtuse and acute angles. The player who finds the most angles wins.

~~ III ~~

TRIANGLES

When you connect straight lines to make a closed two-dimensional shape, the result is a **polygon.** Polygons include squares, triangles, and rectangles, which you probably know a lot about. But they also include pentagons (with five sides), hexagons (with six sides), heptagons (with seven sides), and many more.

Polygons with three sides are some of the most interesting figures in geometry. You probably know that these figures are called triangles. But triangles are not as simple as they first appear. There are many types of triangles. Many of them are named after the types of angles they contain, such as acute, obtuse, and right. There are also scalene and isosceles triangles.

In this section, you'll learn about many of the different kinds of triangles, the exterior and interior angles in a triangle, congruent triangles, and the Pythagorean theorem.

Along the way, you'll make a triangle collage, play triangle memory, put together a triangle puzzle, and use triangles to figure out the heights of objects. Triangles are fascinating. So let's get started!

Triangle Collage

There are six basic types of triangles:

1. **Acute triangle:** *All three angles of an acute triangle are less than 90 degrees.*

2. **Obtuse triangle:** *One angle of an obtuse triangle is greater than 90 degrees.*

3. **Right triangle:** *One angle of a right triangle is equal to 90 degrees.*

4. **Scalene triangle:** *All three sides of a scalene triangle have different measures.*

5. **Isosceles triangle:** *Two angles and two sides of an isosceles triangle are equal.*

6. **Equilateral triangle:** *All three angles and all three sides of an equilateral triangle are equal.*

In this activity, you'll make a poster using all the different triangle types.

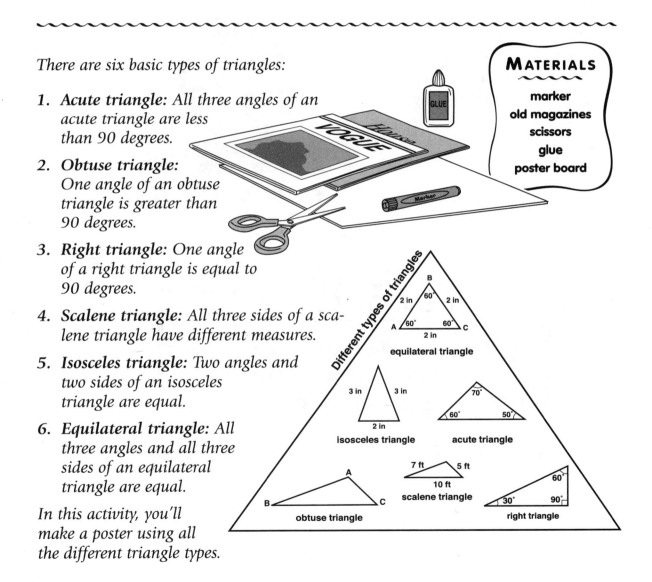

MATERIALS

marker
old magazines
scissors
glue
poster board

Different types of triangles

equilateral triangle
B 60° 2 in, A 60°, 2 in, C 60°, 2 in

isosceles triangle
3 in, 3 in, 2 in

acute triangle
70°, 60°, 50°

obtuse triangle
A, B, C

scalene triangle
7 ft, 5 ft, 10 ft

right triangle
60°, 30°, 90°

25

Procedure

1. Draw at least six large triangles on different magazine pages. Make a picture in the magazine the center of each triangle. For example, you could draw a triangle around a person's face like this:

   Draw one of every type of triangle in the list on page 25.

2. Cut out each triangle.

3. Glue the triangles on the poster board in a way that makes an interesting picture.

isosceles triangle

BRAIN Stretcher

Make another collage out of all right triangles or all obtuse triangles or all equilateral triangles. How does that change the way the collage looks?

Triangle Memory

Play this game to practice matching triangles to their type.

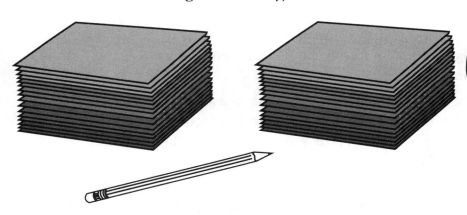

Game Preparation

1. Write one of the following types of triangles on each index card of one color:

Acute triangle	Scalene triangle
Acute triangle	Scalene triangle
Obtuse triangle	Isosceles triangle
Obtuse triangle	Isosceles triangle
Right triangle	Equilateral triangle
Right triangle	Equilateral triangle

2. Write one of the following sets of angle measurements on each index card of the second color.

40-60-80	60-60-60
50-60-70	60-60-60
30-40-110	50-50-80
10-20-150	10-10-170
40-50-90	25-55-100
5-85-90	1-2-177

Game Rules

1. Shuffle the cards of one color together and place them facedown on the table. Do the same for the other color.

2. Player 1 turns over one card of each color. If the measurements on one card match the definition of the type of triangle described on the other card, the player keeps both cards. If they are not a match, Player 1 places them facedown on the table.

3. Player 2 now turns over two cards (one of each color) and tries to find a match. If both cards match, Player 2 gets to keep both cards.

4. When there are no cards left or no more matches on the table, the player with the most cards is the winner.

Triangle Angles

*Use the angles of a triangle as the pieces of a
puzzle and learn something interesting
about the sum of a triangle's angles.*

MATERIALS

pencil
paper
ruler
scissors

Procedure

1. Use a ruler to draw a triangle on a piece of paper.
2. Cut out the triangle.
3. Rip off the three corners of the triangle.
4. Put the three corners in a row so that the angles meet at one point and at least one side of each angle touches the side of another angle.
5. The angles of the triangle should form a straight line. The sum of the angles of your triangle is 180 degrees.

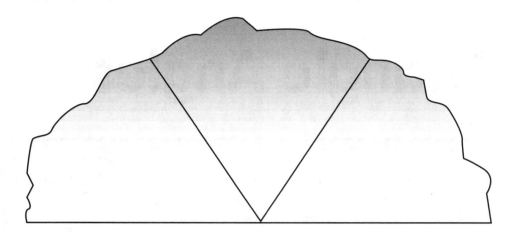

6. Draw another triangle and repeat steps 2 through 5.

BRAIN Stretcher

Can you draw a triangle whose angles do not add up to 180 degrees?

Outside the Triangle

Six exterior angles can be formed outside every triangle. An exterior angle is formed by one side of a triangle and the extension of another side. (See angles 1 through 6 in the figure below.)

Try this activity to learn more about the exterior angles of a triangle.

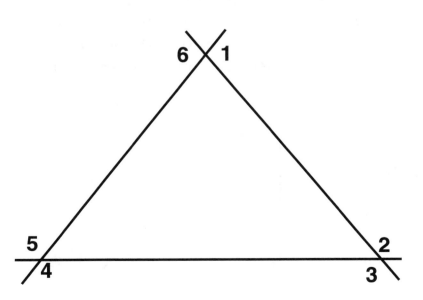

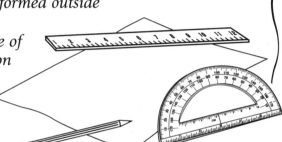

MATERIALS

ruler
pencil
paper
protractor

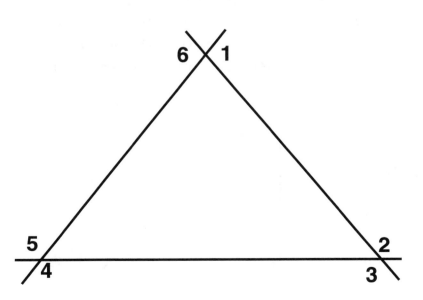

Procedure

1. Use a ruler to draw an acute triangle. Extend one of the sides of the triangle to form an exterior angle.

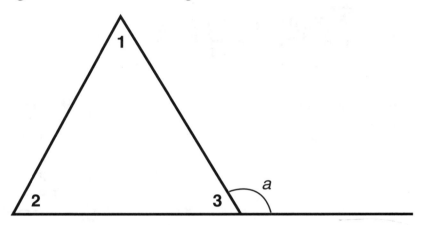

Exterior angle *a* of an acute triangle

2. Label the exterior angle *a*. Label the interior angles 1, 2, and 3. In the triangle shown here, angle *a* is the exterior angle, angle 3 is the adjacent interior angle, and angles 1 and 2 are the nonadjacent interior angles.

3. Use a protractor to measure the exterior angle. Enter this measurement in a chart like the one on page 34.

4. Use a protractor to measure each of the nonadjacent interior angles. Enter these measurements in your chart.

5. Add the measures of angles 1 and 2. Enter the result in your chart.

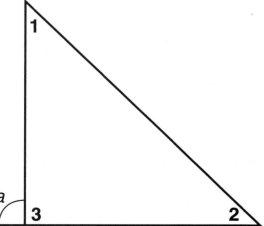

6. Use a ruler to draw a right triangle.

7. Extend one of the sides of the right triangle.

8. Label the exterior angle *a*. Label the interior angles 1, 2, and 3. In the above triangle, angle *a* is the exterior angle, angle 3 is the adjacent interior angle, and angles 1 and 2 are nonadjacent interior angles.

9. Use a protractor to measure the exterior angle. Enter this measurement in your chart.

10. Measure each of the nonadjacent interior angles. Enter these measurements in your chart.

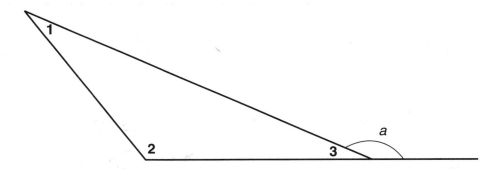

11. Add the measurements of angles 1 and 2. Enter the result in your chart.

12. Draw an obtuse triangle.

13. Extend one of the sides of the obtuse triangle.

14. Label the exterior angle *a*. Label the interior angles 1, 2, and 3. In the above triangle, angle *a* is the exterior angle, angle 3 is the adjacent interior angle, and angles 1 and 2 are the nonadjacent interior angles.

15. Measure the exterior angle. Enter this measurement in your chart.

16. Measure each of the nonadjacent interior angles. Enter these measurements in your chart.

17. Add the measurements of angles 1 and 2. Enter the result in your chart.

Type of Triangle	Measure of Angle a	Measure of Angle 3	Measure of Angle 1	Measure of Angle 2	Sum of Angles 1 + 2

18. Do any two columns of the chart always match? Which ones?

Tips and Tricks

Exterior angle a should always equal the sum of interior angles 1 and 2—that is, any exterior angle of a triangle is equal to the sum of the two nonadjacent interior angles (also known as **remote interior angles**).

BRAIN Stretcher

What is the sum of the six exterior angles of an acute triangle? Draw an acute triangle, measure its exterior angles, and add them together to find out.

Triangle Area

In geometry, **area** is the size of the region enclosed by a figure. Area is usually expressed as a square unit, such as square inches or square centimeters. To find the area of a rectangle, you multiply its length by its width. But how do you find the area of a triangle? Try this activity to see how it's done.

MATERIALS

ruler
pencil
graph paper
colored pencils or crayons
scissors
glue
colored paper

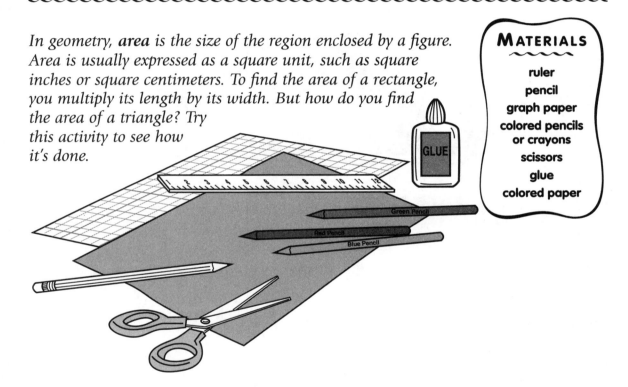

Procedure

1. Use a ruler to help you draw a triangle on graph paper. Make the base of the triangle line up with a line on the graph paper. Begin your base line at the beginning of a square on the graph paper, and end your line at the end of a square. Make sure the top of the triangle comes in contact with a line on the graph paper. Color the triangle with a red pencil.

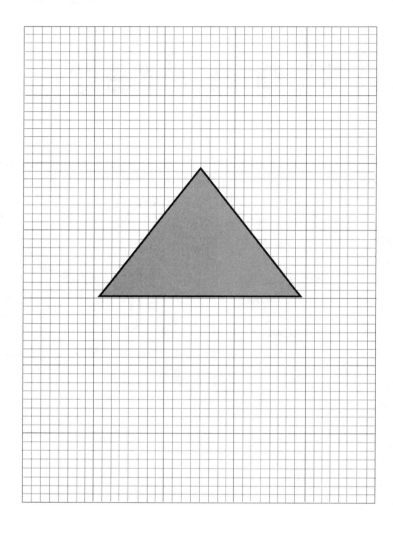

2. Draw a rectangle around the triangle. Use the bottom of the triangle as the bottom of the rectangle. The opposite side of the rectangle should be drawn so that it touches the highest point of the triangle.

3. Try counting the number of squares in the triangle. It's hard because some of the squares are cut off at different points.

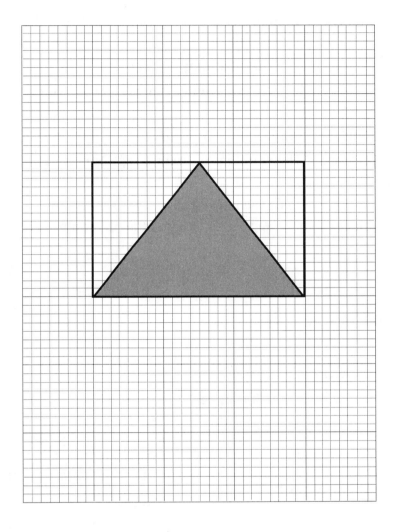

4. Count the number of squares in the rectangle, or multiply the number of squares on the bottom of the rectangle by the number of squares on one side. This is the area of the rectangle.

5. Divide the area of the rectangle by 2 to find the number of squares in the triangle. The triangle covers one-half as many squares as the rectangle does. If we use the graph paper squares as our unit of measurement, then the area of this triangle is equal to the number of squares in the triangle.

6. Draw another triangle of a different size on the graph paper. Color the triangle blue.

7. Repeat steps 2 through 5 to find the area of this triangle.

8. Draw another triangle of a different size on the graph paper. Color the triangle green.

9. Repeat steps 2 through 5 to find the area of this triangle.

10. Cut out all three rectangles. Then cut the colored triangle out of each rectangle.

11. On a piece of colored paper, glue the leftover pieces of each rectangle onto the triangle that was cut from that rectangle. What do you notice?

Tips and Tricks

The formula for the area of a triangle is $\frac{1}{2} \times b \times h$, where b is the base of the triangle and h is the height of the triangle.

Can you see from the activity why this formula works?

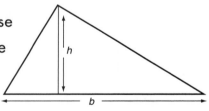

Formula for area of a triangle

area = 1/2 b x h

BRAIN Stretcher

Can you figure out how to find the area of any triangle?

Two the Same

Triangles with the same size and shape are **congruent**. In congruent triangles, the angles and sides are also congruent. Try this activity to make congruent triangles.

MATERIALS

marker
protractor
cardboard
pencil
colored pencils
or crayons
scissors
ruler
straws
paper

Procedure

1. Use a marker and protractor to draw two 15-degree angles on a piece of cardboard. Make the sides of the angles about 2 inches (5 cm) long. Draw an arc at the end of each angle. Write "15 degrees" (15°) in the center of both angles. Color the interior of each 15-degree angle blue. Cut out each of the angles along the sides and along the arc. Each angle should look like a slice of pizza.

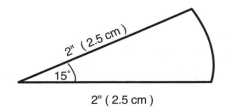

2" (2.5 cm)

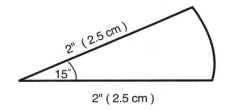

2" (2.5 cm)

2. Use a marker to draw four 30-degree angles on a piece of cardboard. Make the sides of these angles about 2 inches (5 cm) long. Draw an arc at the end of each angle. Write 30 degrees in the center of the angles. Color the interior of each of the 30-degree angles red. Cut out all of these angles along the sides and along the arc.

3. Draw four 45-degree angles in the same way that you drew all the other angles. Color them green.

4. Draw four 60-degree angles. Color them orange.

5. Draw two 90-degree angles. Color them brown.

6. Draw two 120-degree angles. Color them purple.

7. Cut out all the angles you made in steps 1 through 6.

8. Measure and cut six straws so that they are each 3 inches (7.5 cm) long.

9. Measure and cut six straws so that they are each 4 inches (10 cm) long.

10. Measure and cut six straws so that they are each 5 inches (12.5 cm) long.

11. Measure and cut six straws so that they are each 6 inches (15 cm) long.

12. Measure and cut six straws so that they are each 7 inches (17.5 cm) long.

13. Measure and cut six straws so that they are each 8 inches (20 cm) long.

14. Take any three straws and make a triangle.

15. Now take three straws of the exact same length and make a second triangle. Does this triangle have the exact same size and shape as the original triangle? Can you construct a triangle that is different from the original triangle? If you match three sides of one triangle to three sides of another triangle, are the triangles *always* the same (congruent)? Enter your answer in a chart like the one on page 41.

16. Now take three of the angles you made in steps 1 through 7 and any three straws and make a triangle. (Make sure the measurements of the angles you use total 180 degrees or you will not be able to form a triangle.) Take three angles that have the exact same measurement as the first three angles and construct a second triangle using straws. If you match

three angles of one triangle to three angles of another triangle, are the triangles *always* the same (congruent)? Enter the answer in your chart.

17. Use the straw pieces and angles to make triangle pairs according to the rest of the matching tests listed in the chart. For each pair, answer the question, Are the two triangles formed always congruent?

Triangle Parts Matched	Are the Two Triangles Formed Always Congruent?
3 sides	[answer to step 15]
3 angles	[answer to step 16]
2 angles	
2 sides	
2 sides and 1 angle	
2 angles and 1 side	
2 angles and 2 sides	
1 angle and 1 side	

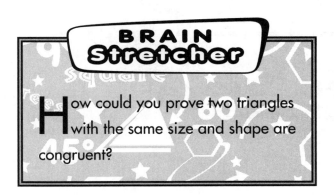

BRAIN Stretcher

How could you prove two triangles with the same size and shape are congruent?

How Tall?

Similar triangles *are triangles that are in the same proportion to each other even if they are different sizes. In* proportion *means that the corresponding angles are equal. In this activity, you will use shadows and similar triangles to figure out how tall things are.*

Procedure

1. Place the salt shaker, soda can, and milk carton on a table.

2. Use a ruler to measure the heights of the salt shaker, soda can, and milk carton in inches or centimeters. Enter the measurements in a chart like the one on page 43.

3. Place a lamp behind the items on the table.

4. Measure the shadow on the table cast by each of the items. Enter the results in your chart.

	Height of Item (inches or cm)	Length of Shadow (inches or cm)	Length of Shadow Divided by Length of Item (inches or cm)
Salt shaker			
Soda can			
Milk carton			

5. Use a calculator to divide the length of the shadow of each item by the height of the item. What do you notice?

6. Cut and tape a piece of string from the top of each object to the end of its shadow. You have formed three similar triangles.

7. Measure the angles of each triangle to prove that they are similar.

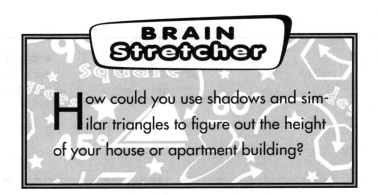

BRAIN Stretcher

How could you use shadows and similar triangles to figure out the height of your house or apartment building?

Perfect Squares

Pythagoras, an early Greek mathematician, gave the world a famous theorem that has to do with triangles. The **Pythagorean theorem** states that the sum of the squares of the legs of a right triangle is equal to the square of the hypotenuse. The **hypotenuse** is the side of the triangle opposite the right angle. The **legs** are the sides adjacent to the right angle. **Squaring** means to multiply the number by itself. So the Pythagorean theorem means that if you know the lengths of the legs of a right triangle, you can figure out the length of the hypotenuse. Here's how:

MATERIALS

calculator
pencil
paper

1. Square the lengths of each leg of the right triangle.

2. Add the squares of the legs together.

3. Find the square root of the sums of the legs. (The square root of a number is the number that when multiplied by itself results in the original number.)

Try this activity to find triangles that fit the Pythagorean theorem.

Procedure

1. Use a calculator to square the numbers from 1 to 20. Enter the results in a chart like the one below. (The first three have been done for you.)

Number	Square
1	1
2	4
3	9
4	
5	
6	
7	
8	
9	
10	
11	
12	
13	
14	
15	
16	
17	
18	
19	
20	

The numbers you get: 1, 4, 9, 16, and 25, . . . are called perfect squares.

2. Place the perfect squares you found in step 1 along the top row and the left column of a chart like the one below.

	1	4	9	16	25														
1	2	5	10	17	26														
4	5	8	13	20	29														
9																			
16																			
25																			

3. Add each pair of perfect squares together. Place the sum of the two numbers in the box where the number along the top row and the number in the left column meet in the grid. Circle any new numbers that fit the definition of a perfect square. How many new perfect squares were created?

4. Because you added two perfect squares together, you can use these new perfect squares to form new right triangles. To do that, take the square root of each of the numbers using a calculator. The answers are the measurements of the sides of the triangles. Then take the square root of the sum of the perfect squares. This is the hypotenuse of the triangle.

EXAMPLE ～～～～～～～～～～～～～～～～～～～～～～～

Notice that on the chart 9 + 16 = 25. Take the square root of all three of these perfect squares. You get 3, 4, and 5. The lengths of the legs of the right triangle are 3 and 4. And 5 is the length of the hypotenuse of the right triangle.

5. Check your calculations by drawing right triangles with the correct measurements.

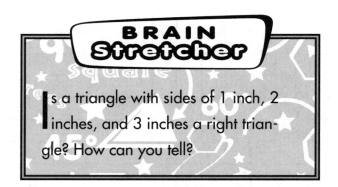

BRAIN Stretcher

Is a triangle with sides of 1 inch, 2 inches, and 3 inches a right triangle? How can you tell?

Pythagorean Proof

Look at the right triangle below. According to the Pythagorean theorem, the squares of the two legs of the triangle equal the square of the hypotenuse, so $a^2 + b^2 = c^2$. Try this puzzle activity to see why this is true.

MATERIALS

graph paper
pencil
ruler
scissors
glue

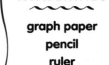
GLUE

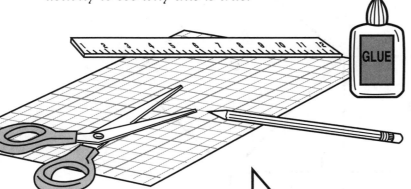

Procedure

1. In the center of the graph paper, use a ruler to draw a right triangle with one leg that is 4 squares long and another leg that is 3 squares long. Label the first leg *a*, the second leg *b*, and the hypotenuse *c*.

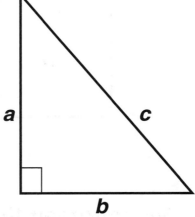

a   *c*

b

right triangle

2. Using the 4-square leg of the triangle as one side, draw a square facing away from the triangle. Label this square a^2. (Remember that the area of a square is the square of one of its sides.)

3. Make another square coming off of the 3-square leg of the triangle. Label this square b^2.

4. Use the ruler to measure side c of the triangle. Use this measurement to make a square that has the hypotenuse of the triangle as one side. Label this square c^2.

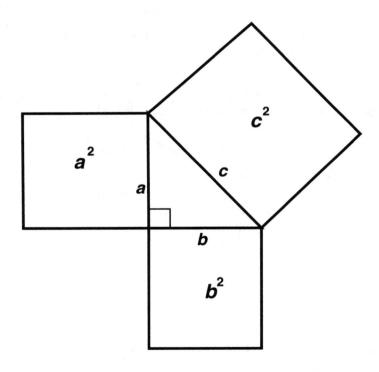

Pythagorean theorem

5. Cut the squares off of the triangle.

6. Place the a^2 square on top of the c^2 square, matching up the corners, and glue it down.

7. Cut the b^2 square into the nine smaller grid squares. Fit these small squares into the remaining space on the figure c^2 and glue them down. Can you see why the sum of the square of the legs equals the square of the hypotenuse in a right triangle?

~~ IV ~~

QUADRILATERALS

Quadrilaterals are four-sided figures. A square and a rectangle are both quadrilaterals, of course. But there are other types of quadrilaterals you may not have heard of.

In this section, you'll learn about the different kinds of quadrilaterals, such as rhombuses and parallelograms, about the angles in quadrilaterals, about the perimeter and area of quadrilaterals, and more.

As you're learning, you'll be playing a quadrilateral memory game, using string and thumbtacks to create a variety of quadrilaterals with the same perimeter, and magically transforming parallelograms into rectangles.

After you finish the activities in this section, you'll start seeing quadrilaterals everywhere and understanding them better.

17

Crazy about Quadrilaterals

There are six basic types of quadrilaterals: parallelograms, rectangles, rhombuses, squares, kites, and trapezoids. Here's how to tell these quadrilaterals apart:

1. A **parallelogram** is a four-sided figure with two pairs of parallel sides.

2. A **rectangle** is a parallelogram with a right angle.

3. A **rhombus** is a parallelogram whose sides are all equal.

4. A **square** is a rhombus with a right angle.

5. A **kite** is a quadrilateral with two pairs of equal and adjacent sides.

6. A **trapezoid** is a quadrilateral with only two parallel sides.

Play this fun matching game to practice remembering which quadrilateral is which.

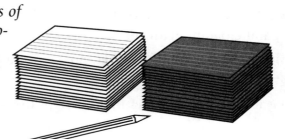

Six Quadrilateral Types

parallelogram

rectangle

rhombus

square

kite

trapezoid

Game Preparation

1. Write the word *square* at the top of one index card and draw a square below it.

2. Write the word *rectangle* at the top of another index card in the same color and draw a rectangle below it.

3. Write the word *rhombus* at the top of another index card in the same color and draw a rhombus below it.

4. Write the word *parallelogram* at the top of another index card in the same color and draw a parallelogram below it.

5. Write the word *trapezoid* at the top of another index card in the same color and draw a trapezoid below it.

6. Write the word *kite* at the top of another index card in the same color and draw a kite below it.

7. Write one of the following definitions on each of the second color of index cards:

    a four-sided figure with two pairs of parallel sides

    a parallelogram with a right angle

    a parallelogram whose sides are all equal

    a rhombus with a right angle

    a quadrilateral with two pairs of equal and adjacent sides

    a quadrilateral with only two parallel sides

Game Rules

1. Shuffle the index cards for each color separately and turn them facedown in two piles.

2. Player 1 turns over one card of each color. If the shape card matches the description card, Player 1 gets to keep both cards. Next, Player 2 takes a turn. If the cards don't match, they should be turned over and shuffled in each stack.

3. Play continues until all matches are found. The winner is the player who has the most cards at the end of the game.

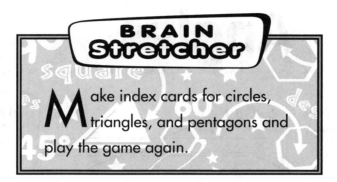

BRAIN Stretcher

Make index cards for circles, triangles, and pentagons and play the game again.

18 Quadrilateral Angles

Quadrilaterals all have four sides, but is there any other way in which they are all alike? Discover the answer by doing this activity.

MATERIALS

protractor
pencil
paper
ruler

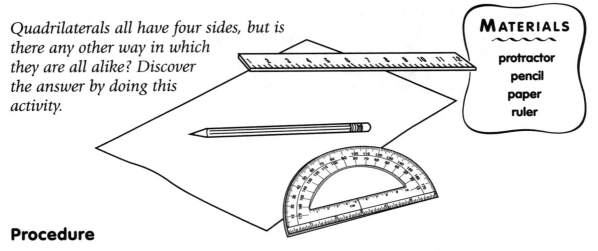

Procedure

1. Use a protractor to measure each of the four angles in each of these quadrilaterals. Enter the results in a chart like the one on page 59.

square

rhombus

rectangle

parallelogram

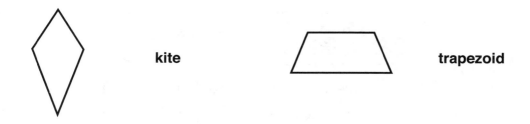

kite

trapezoid

	Angle 1	Angle 2	Angle 3	Angle 4	Angle 1 + Angle 2 + Angle 3 + Angle 4 +
Square					
Rectangle					
Parallelogram					
Rhombus					
Kite					
Trapezoid					

2. Add all four angles of each quadrilateral and write the answer in the last column of your chart. What do you notice about the sums of the angles in these quadrilaterals?

3. Use a ruler to draw your own four-sided figure of any shape. What is the sum of the angles of the figure you drew? Draw another four-sided figure. What is the sum of the angles of this figure? What do the answers tell you about quadrilaterals?

BRAIN Stretcher

1. What is the largest angle in any of the quadrilaterals drawn? What is the largest possible angle a quadrilateral could contain?

2. What is the smallest angle in any of the quadrilaterals drawn? What is the smallest possible angle a quadrilateral could contain?

3. A pentagon is a five-sided figure (with five angles). What is the sum of the angles of a pentagon? Do you think the total number of degrees in the angles of every pentagon is the same?

String Shapes

*The **perimeter** of a figure is the distance around its boundary. Quadrilaterals with different shapes can have the same perimeter measurements. Try this activity to see how.*

MATERIALS

scissors

long piece of string

ruler

large piece of cardboard

20 push pins or thumbtacks

marker

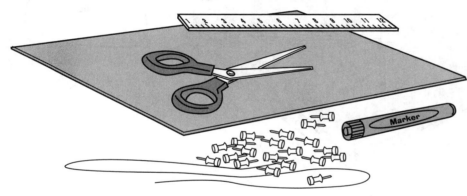

Procedure

1. Cut the string into five 10-inch (25-cm) pieces. Use a ruler to check the measurements.

2. Tie the ends of each piece of string together to form large circles of string.

3. Form a circle with one piece of string on a piece of cardboard. Make the circle into a square by pulling the sides of the string tight with the push pins. (Use the push pins as the corners of the square.)

4. Use the remaining pieces of string and push pins to form a rectangle, a parallelogram, a rhombus, and a trapezoid.

5. Label each type of quadrilateral and write the perimeter of each quadrilateral inside the figure.

Double It!

See what happens to the area of a square when you double the sides.

Procedure

1. With a ruler, draw a square with sides that measure 2 inches (5 cm).

2. Draw a line down the center of both sides of the square, dividing the square into 1-inch (2.5-cm) squares. Your square should look like this:

3. Count the number of small squares formed. Enter the results in a chart like the one on page 63. This is the area of the square.

4. Draw a square with 3-inch (7.5-cm) sides.

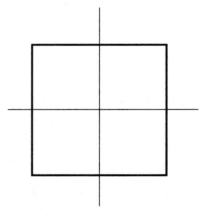

2" square divided into four squares

5. Divide this square into 1-inch (2.5-cm) squares. How many 1-inch (2.5-cm) squares are in this large square? Enter the results in your chart. This is the area of the square in square units.

6. Draw a square with 4-inch (10-cm) sides.

7. Divide this square into 1-inch (2.5-cm) squares. How many 1-inch (2.5-cm) squares are in this large square? Enter the results in your chart.

8. Draw a square with 6-inch (15-cm) sides.

9. Use a pencil and ruler to divide this square into 1-inch (2.5-cm) squares. How many 1-inch (2.5-cm) squares are in this large square? Enter the results in your chart.

10. What happens to the area of a square when you double the length of its sides? Is the area doubled?

Length of Side of Square	Area of Square (square inches or square cm)
2 inches (5 cm)	
3 inches (7.5 cm)	
4 inches (10 cm)	
6 inches (15 cm)	
8 inches (20 cm)	

To find out, divide the area of a 4-inch (10-cm) square by the area of a 2-inch (5-cm) square. Next, divide the area of a 6-inch (15-cm) square by the area of a 3-inch (7.5-cm) square. Finally, divide the area of an 8-inch (20-cm) square by the area of a 4-inch (10-cm) square. If you double the length of a side of a square, the area of the square increases by how many times?

BRAIN Stretcher

What happens to the area of a square if you triple the length of the sides? How does the area of a square with 2-inch (5-cm) sides compare to the area of a square with 6-inch (15-cm) sides?

Rectangle Race

To find the area of a rectangle, multiply the length of the rectangle by its width. Play this game to practice finding the area of rectangles.

MATERIALS

2 players
pencil
graph paper
scissors
jar

Game Preparation

1. On graph paper draw rectangles with the following dimensions:

   5 boxes long and 3 boxes wide

   6 boxes long and 4 boxes wide

   12 boxes long and 2 boxes wide

   8 boxes long and 3 boxes wide

   20 boxes long and 1 box wide

   5 boxes long and 4 boxes wide

   10 boxes long and 2 boxes wide

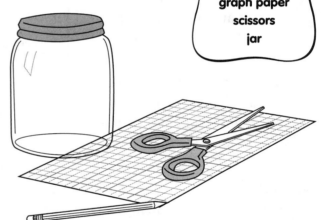

2. Cut out each rectangle, fold it up, and put it in a jar.

Game Rules

1. Player 1 picks a rectangle out of the jar and calls out the dimensions in boxes called units.

2. Both players try to calculate the area of the rectangle in square units. Whoever shouts out the correct answer first gets a point.

3. To confirm that the answer is correct, the players count the number of boxes in the rectangle.

4. Players take turns pulling rectangles out of the jar and calling out the dimensions until all of the rectangles have been used. The winner is the player with the most points at the end of the game.

BRAIN Stretcher

What did you notice about the areas of the rectangles? How many different rectangles can you draw with areas of 12 square units? (Each square of the graph paper is a square unit.) How many different rectangles can you draw with areas of 100 square units?

22

Parallelogram Presto Change-O

Try this activity to change a parallelogram into a rectangle; then find out why this makes it easy to find a parallelogram's area.

MATERIALS

pencil
paper
scissors
tape
ruler

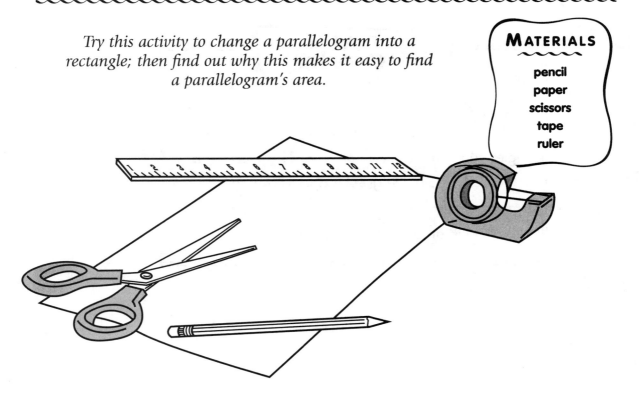

Procedure

1. Draw a parallelogram on a piece of paper.

2. Draw a perpendicular line from one of the vertices of the parallelogram to the opposite side. (**Vertices** is the plural of vertex. A **vertex** is a point where two line segments meet.)

3. Cut out the triangle formed by the perpendicular line.

4. Place the triangle you cut from one end of the parallelogram on the other end of the parallelogram to form a rectangle and tape the pieces together.

5. Find the area of the rectangle you formed. First use a ruler to measure the length of the rectangle's sides. Then multiply the length of the rectangle by its width to find its area.

6. The area of the parallelogram you drew is the same as the area of the rectangle you created.

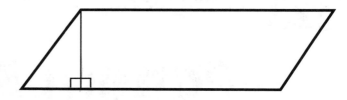

Parallelogram with perpendicular line drawn from one of the vertices to the other side

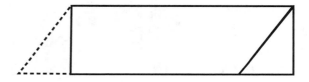

Place the triangle you cut from one end of the parallelogram on the other end of the parallelogram to form a rectangle and tape the pieces together

Tips and Tricks

To find the area of a parallelogram without cutting and pasting, just multiply the width times the height.

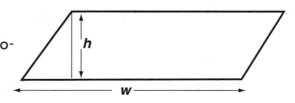

Parallelogram width and height

23

Pattern Blocks

A **rhombus** is a four-sided figure in which all the sides are of equal lengths. This sounds like a square, right? A square is a special kind of rhombus that has right angles. Other rhombus shapes—the ones that don't have right angles— look sort of like squashed squares.

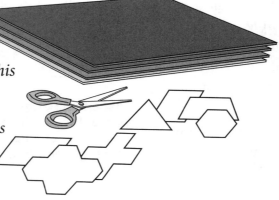

rhombus

A trapezoid is a four-sided figure that has just one pair of parallel sides.

trapezoid

In this activity, you'll use rhombuses, trapezoids, and other shapes as tiles to make patterns.

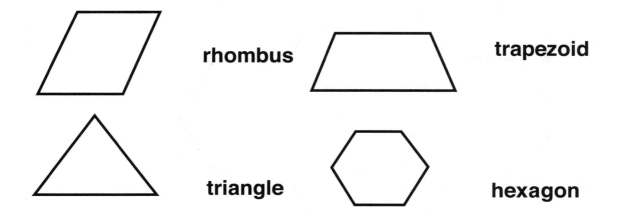

rhombus

trapezoid

triangle

hexagon

Procedure

1. Photocopy and cut out the tile templates above.

2. Use each template to trace the shapes on the poster board. Each shape should have its own color (for example, all rhombuses are blue, all triangles are red, etc.) Make 20 copies of each shape.

3. Photocopy the shape patterns on this page and page 70.

4. Use the different-shaped tiles to completely fill in each shape pattern without overlapping. How many different combinations of tiles can you find that work for each shape?

5. Use the tiles to make up your own patterns.

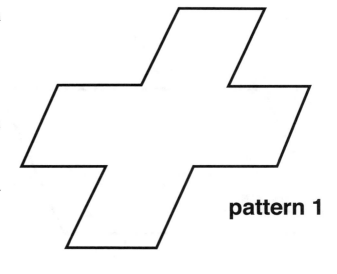

pattern 1

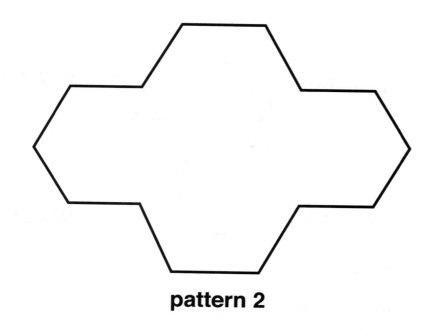

pattern 2

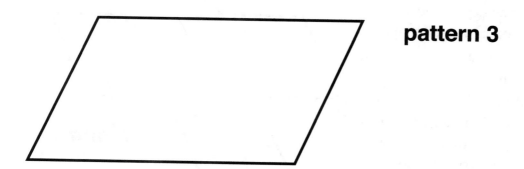

pattern 3

Shape Storybook

In addition to triangles and quadrilaterals, there are many other polygons with more than four sides. For example, there are **pentagons** (five-sided figures), **hexagons** (six-sided figures), **heptagons** (seven-sided figures), **octagons** (eight-sided figures), **nonagons** (nine-sided figures), and **decagons** (ten-sided figures). In this activity, you'll write a story and illustrate it with figures that have more than four sides.

MATERIALS

colored construction paper

ruler

pencil

scissors

white paper

crayons or colored pencils

paper brad

Procedure

1. Pick any one of the many-sided figures listed above.

2. Fold a piece of construction paper in half and use the ruler and pencil to draw a figure of the type you chose on the construction paper.

3. Cut around the figure through both layers of construction paper so that you have two pieces of the same shape.

4. Use the construction-paper shape you made to trace the shape on several pieces of drawing paper. Cut out these pieces of paper.

5. On the white paper, use crayons or colored pencils to write and illustrate a story in which there are no squares, triangles, or circles. Instead, everything is made out of hexagons, heptagons, and other figures that have more than four sides.

6. When you're finished illustrating your story, put the white paper between the construction-paper shapes and fasten the pages together with a paper brad.

~~~ V ~~~
CIRCLES

A **circle** has no beginning and no end, but it does have an origin, a radius, a diameter, and a circumference. In this section you'll learn about these parts of a circle, plus you'll learn to measure the radius and diameter of circles, determine the value of pi, and discover the number of degrees in a circle. You'll also get to make a drawing compass, calculate the circumference of the tires on your bicycle, and figure out how much area of a pizza you can eat.

Around and Around

In a circle, the distance around the perimeter is called the **circumference**, the distance across the middle of the circle is called the **diameter**, and the center point is called the **origin**. The distance from the origin to any point on the circumference is called the **radius**. This activity shows you how to create perfect circles with a pencil, a paper clip, and a piece of string.

MATERIALS

2 paper clips

piece of string
5 inches
(12.5 cm) long

2 pencils

paper

piece of string
7 inches
(17.5 cm) long

Procedure

1. Unbend the tip of a paper clip.

2. Tie one end of the 5-inch (12.5-cm) piece of string tightly around the paper clip and bend the end of the paper clip back to hold the string in place.

3. Tie the other end of the string around a pencil. You have made a drawing compass that will make circles with a radius of 5 inches (12.5 cm).

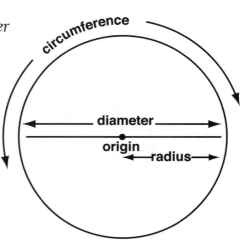

Parts of a circle

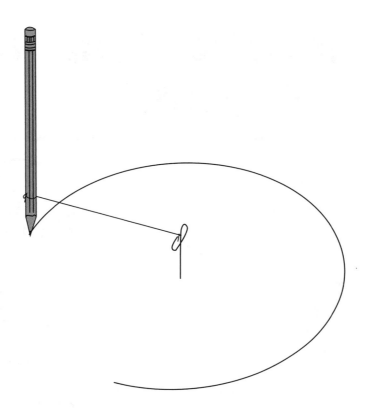

Using the drawing compass to make a circle

4. To use your compass, place the point of the paper clip in the center of a piece of paper.

5. Holding the paper clip down and keeping the string stretched tightly, draw a circle by moving the pencil around the paper clip.

6. Tie the 7-inch (17.5-cm) piece of string to the other pencil and paper clip. You have made a drawing compass that will make circles with a radius of 7 inches (17.5 cm).

7. Measure the diameters of the circles you drew. How do they compare with the lengths of the strings you used to draw the circles?

Finding Pi

The relationship between the circumference and the diameter of a circle is a very special one, as the ancient Babylonians, Egyptians, and Greeks all discovered. Try this activity to learn about that relationship.

MATERIALS

plate, saucer, cup, glass, garbage pail, quarter, and other round items you can find around your home

string

ruler

pencil

paper

calculator

Procedure

1. Find the circumference of each round object by placing a string around each object (for cups, glasses, etc., put the string around the top rim). Remove the string, and using a ruler, measure the length of string used to circle each item. Write your findings in a chart like the one on page 78.

2. Measure the diameter of each item using the ruler. Make sure that your ruler rests across the center of the circle when you take your measurements. Write your findings in your chart.

3. Use a calculator to divide the circumference of each circle by the diameter of the circle. Write the results in your chart.

4. Compare the results in column 4 for each item.

Round Item	Circumference	Diameter	Circumference/Diameter
Glass			
Cup			
Saucer			
Plate			
Garbage pail			

5. How can you use the results to find the circumference of any circle?

Tips and Tricks

The relationship you discovered is that the circumference of a circle divided by its diameter is always the same number. The Greeks called this number pi (π). The value of pi is about 3.14, but pi is an irrational number, which means that it can never be completely calculated because the digits after the decimal point go on forever.

BRAIN Stretcher

If the diameter of one circle is twice as large as that of another circle, what do you think the relationship between the circumferences of these two circles might be?

Bicycle Odometer

Use pi to calculate the circumference of a bicycle tire; then use the circumference to figure out how far your bicycle would have gone if the tire made 100 revolutions.

MATERIALS

tape measure
bicycle
pencil
paper
calculator

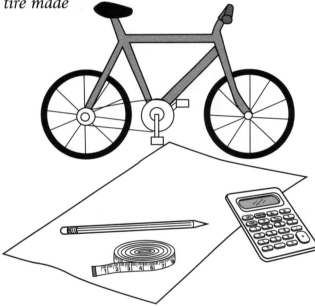

Procedure

1. Measure the diameter of one tire on your bicycle.

2. Calculate the circumference of your bicycle tire. Multiply pi (3.14) by the diameter of the tire. (Use a calculator if you need help.)

3. Now measure the circumference of the tire of your bicycle. Are the two measures the same?

4. How far would you have traveled if the tire of your bicycle made 100 revolutions?

Circle Area

Here's a way to approximate the area of a circle.

MATERIALS

graph paper
pencil
plate
saucer

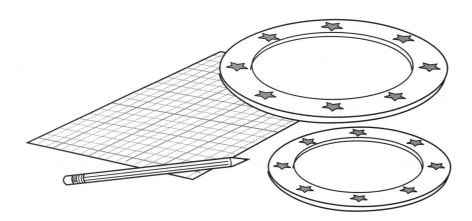

Procedure

1. Draw a circle on a piece of graph paper using a plate as your guide. Try to position the edges of the plate along the lines printed on the graph paper.

2. What is the diameter of the circle? Count the number of boxes that cross the center of the circle and put the answer in a chart like the one on page 82.

3. What is the radius of the circle? (The radius is one-half of the diameter.) Write the answer in your chart.

4. Count the number of complete squares inside the circle. Put an X on each square you count to make sure you don't count the same square twice. Write this number down.

5. Count the number of partial squares inside the circle. Shade each of these partial squares with your pencil. Multiply the number of partial squares by $\frac{1}{2}$. Write this number down.

6. Add the numbers in steps 4 and 5 to find the approximate area of the circle in square units. Write this number in your chart.

7. Repeat steps 1 through 6 using a saucer to make the circle.

8. What is the relationship between the area of each circle and its diameter? Divide the measurements and enter the results in your chart.

9. What is the relationship between the area of each circle and its radius? Divide the measurements and enter the results in your chart.

	Diameter	Radius	Approximate Area	Area/ Diameter	Area/Radius
Large circle (plate)					
Small circle (saucer)					

Tips and Tricks

To check your approximation, draw a square around the circle that touches the circle on all four sides. Determine the length of one side of the square by counting the boxes. Find the area of the square by multiplying the length of this side by itself. The area of the circle should be less than the area of the square.

Pizza Party

The basic formula for finding the area of a circle is πr^2, where π is pi and r is the radius of a circle. To calculate the area from the diameter, you just need to divide the diameter by 2 to get the radius, then square the radius (multiply it by itself) and multiply the result by pi (3.14). Try this activity to determine the area of part of a circle and see how much pizza your family can eat.

Procedure

1. Call a pizza parlor and ask for the diameter of the different-size pizzas they sell. Also ask for the number of slices in each size pizza. Enter the results in a chart like the one on page 84.

2. Using the diameter and the formula πr^2, calculate the area of a small pizza. Enter the results in your chart.

3. Now calculate the area of a single slice of a small pizza by dividing the area of the whole pizza by the number of slices. Enter the results in your chart.

4. Calculate the area of a large pizza and enter the results in your chart.

5. Calculate the area of a single slice of a large pizza and enter the results in your chart.

Pizza Size	Number of Slices	Diameter of Pizza	Total Area of Pizza (πr^2)	Area per Slice
Small pizza				
Large pizza				

6. List the names of the members of your family in a chart like the one on page 85.

7. Ask the members of your family how many slices of pizza they would eat if you ordered a large pizza. Enter the results in your chart.

8. Ask the members of your family how many slices of pizza they would eat if you ordered a small pizza. Enter the results in your chart.

9. Multiply the number of slices of a small pizza that each person would eat by the area of a single slice of a small pizza. Enter the results in your chart.

10. Multiply the number of slices of a large pizza that each person would eat by the area of a single slice of a large pizza. Enter the results in your chart.

Family Member	Number of Small Slices He or She Would Eat	Area of Single Small Slice	Total Area of Small Slices He or She Would Eat	Number of Larger Slices He or She Would Eat	Area of Single Large Slice	Total Area of Larger Slices He or She Would Eat

11. Who has the biggest appetite for pizza?

Central Angles

How many degrees around is a full circle?

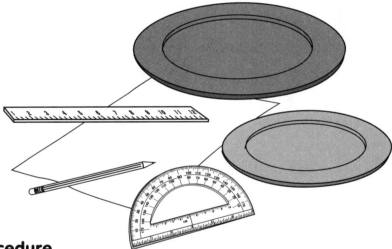

Procedure

1. Trace a plate on a sheet of paper to form a circle.

2. Using a ruler, draw a line through the center of the circle.

3. Draw a second line through the center of the circle. This second line can be as near to or far away from the first as you would like.

4. Using a protractor, measure the four central angles formed. Enter the results in a chart like the one on page 87.

5. Trace the saucer to form a circle. Draw two different lines through the center of the circle.

6. Using a protractor, measure the four central angles formed. Enter the results in your chart.

	Plate	Saucer
Angle 1		
Angle 2		
Angle 3		
Angle 4		
Total degrees in circle		

7. Add the total number of degrees in each circle.

BRAIN Stretcher

Draw three lines through each center of two different circles. Measure the angles formed. What is the sum of the measures of the angles in each circle? Now draw four lines through the center of another circle and measure the angles. What do you notice?

~~~ VI ~~~

SOLIDS

Solids are three-dimensional geometric figures. Some examples are spheres, cylinders, pyramids, cubes, and prisms. Instead of just width and height, three-dimensional figures have three measurements: length, width, and height. Any flat surface on a solid is called a **face,** a line segment where two faces meet is called an **edge,** and a corner where three or more edges meet is called a **vertex. A polyhedron** is a three-dimensional shape with faces that are polygons. Cubes, pyramids, and prisms are all poly-hedrons (or polyhedra). Cylinders, cones, and spheres are three-dimensional curved shapes.

In this section, you'll learn about some of the different solid shapes and their characteristics, how to find the surface area and volume of some solids, and how to compare solids that have the same volume but different shapes. Along the way, you'll make clay models, use building blocks to make differ-ent rectangular solids, and make a three-dimensional figure from a two-dimensional pattern.

Solid Shapes

Try this activity to make models of different solid shapes.

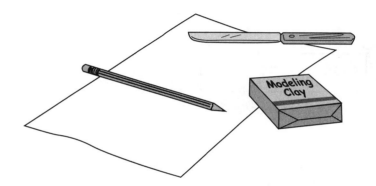

Procedure

1. Make seven balls of clay. Each ball of clay should be exactly the same size. Therefore, they will all have the same volume.

2. Use each of the balls of clay to make one of the following three-dimensional shapes. Use the diagrams for help.

Cube

Rectangular solid

Cone

Cylinder

Pyramid with triangular base

Pyramid with square base

Sphere

Three-Dimensional Shapes

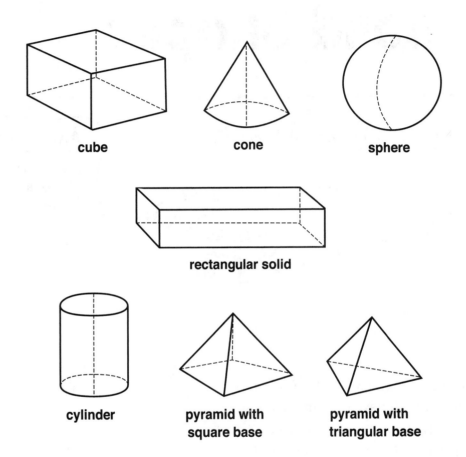

cube   cone   sphere

rectangular solid

cylinder   pyramid with   pyramid with
              square base   triangular base

3. We know that each of the shapes has approximately the same volume, but which looks the largest? Which looks the smallest?

4. Print the name of each shape in large letters on seven separate sheets of paper.

5. Without referring to the book, put each model on the correctly labeled piece of paper.

1. Use the knife to slice each shape in half with a horizontal cut across the center of each shape. What new shapes did you create?

2. Put each of the shapes back together.

3. Cut each shape in half with a vertical cut down the center of each shape. What new shapes did you create?

Cereal Surfaces

*The **surface area** of a solid is the total area of the solid's faces. Cut up an old cereal box to find out how to calculate the surface area of a rectangular solid.*

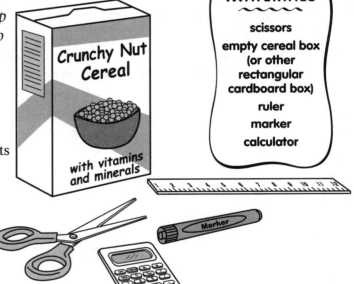

Procedure

1. Cut the cereal box along each of its edges to create six rectangles.

2. Measure the length and width of each of the sides of the rectangle. Write the measurements on the back of each rectangle using a marker.

3. Use the calculator to compute the area of each of these rectangles. Change the measurements to decimals, then multiply the length of each rectangle by its width.

4. Add the areas of all six rectangles to get the total surface area of the cereal box.

5. Find another food box in your kitchen. This time try to measure the surface area of the box without cutting it up.

6. Which box looks bigger? Which box has the greatest surface area?

Cylinder Surfaces

How do you find the surface area of a curved solid, such as a cylinder? Try this activity to find one way.

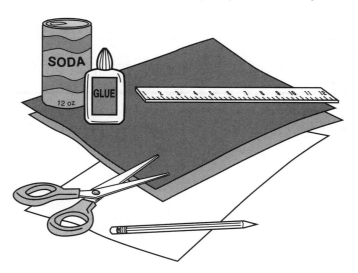

Procedure

1. Trace the bottom of a soda can on a piece of colored paper. Cut out the circle you drew.

2. Trace the top of a soda can on a piece of colored paper. Cut out the circle you drew.

3. Measure the height of the soda can.

4. Cut a rectangle out of a sheet of colored paper. The rectangle should be 11 inches (28 cm) long and the same height as the soda can.

5. Wrap the paper rectangle around the soda can until it exactly covers the sides of the can. Cut off any excess paper.

6. Glue your three cutouts to a piece of white paper. At the top of this piece of paper write "Surface Area of a Soda Can."

7. Calculate the area of each of these three shapes. Enter the results in a chart like the one below.

	Area (in square inches or square centimeters)
Area of top of soda can	
Area of bottom of soda can	
Area of sides of soda can	
Total surface area of soda can	

8. Add the area of the two circles and the rectangle together to find the total surface area of the soda can.

Cube Construction

*Try this activity to find out how to calculate
the volume of a cube.*

Procedure

1. Draw the following diagram on a sheet of paper. The sides of each of the squares should be exactly 1 inch long.

2. Cut out this diagram and tape the edges together to form a 1-inch cube. A 1-inch cube has a length of 1 inch, a width of 1 inch, and a height of 1 inch.

cube pattern

3. Repeat steps 1 and 2 ten times to make a total of ten 1-inch cubes.

4. Now put some of the 1-inch cubes together to create a cube that is 2 inches long, 2 inches wide, and 2 inches tall.

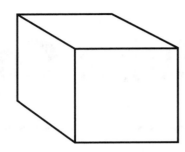

5. How many 1-inch cubes did it take to make a 2-inch cube? It should have taken you eight 1-inch cubes. There are 8 cubic inches in a 2-inch cube. This is the volume of the cube.

finished cube

6. To do this activity in centimeters, follow steps 1 through 5 with a 1-centimeter cube instead of a 1-inch cube. How many cubic centimeters are in a 2-centimeter cube?

7. Use the 1-inch (or 1-centimeter) cube to figure out how many cubic inches (or cubic centimeters) are in a cube with 3-inch (or 3-centimeter) sides.

8. How many cubic inches (or centimeters) are in a cube with 4-inch (or 4-centimeter) sides?

Tips and Tricks

To find the volume of a cube, multiply the length by the width by the height—that is, you just cube (multiply a number by itself three times) the measurement of one side. The volume of a 2-inch cube is 2 × 2 × 2, which equals 8 cubic inches.

Volume of a Cylinder

Use sand and cubes to compute the volume of a cylinder.

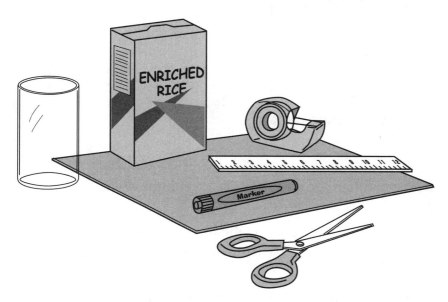

Procedure

1. Draw the pattern shown on page 100 on a piece of cardboard and cut it out. Make sure the sides are exactly 1 inch (2.5 cm) long. Fold the pattern into a cube with one open side and tape the edges together.

2. Fill the cardboard cube exactly to the top with sand or rice.

3. Pour the cardboard cube of sand or rice into the glass. Keep filling up the cube and pouring the contents into the glass until it is full. How many

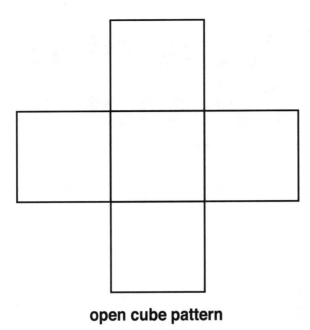

open cube pattern

cubes of rice does it take to fill up the glass? This is the volume of the glass in cubic inches.

4. Now use a ruler to measure the distance across the base of the glass. This is the diameter of the base of the cylinder. Divide this number by 2 to get the radius of the cylinder.

5. Use the radius of the base of the glass to calculate the volume of the glass in cubic inches. Just multiply the radius times itself and multiply the answer times 3.14 (π). Multiply the answer to this equation by the height of the glass: volume = r^2 (π)(h). How does your result compare to the result you got in step 3?

6. Find four other glasses of different sizes. Repeat steps 2 through 5.

Building Blocks

*Make rectangular solids with
the same volume but different shapes.*

MATERIALS

paper
pencil
**36 cubes of any
type (blocks,
sugar cubes,
paper cubes, etc.)**

Procedure

1. You can make four different rectangular solids that each contain exactly
12 cubes. Try it and see! Use 12 cubes to construct each of the following
rectangular solids:

Width 1 cube, height 2 cubes, length 6 cubes

Width 3 cubes, height 1 cube, length 4 cubes

Width 2 cubes, height 2 cubes, length 3 cubes

Width 1 cube, height 1 cube, length 12 cubes

2. How many different rectangular solids can you construct with exactly 8 cubes? What are their dimensions?

3. How many different rectangular solids can you construct with exactly 20 cubes? What are their dimensions?

4. How many different rectangular solids can you construct with exactly 24 cubes? What are their dimensions?

5. How many different rectangular solids can you construct with exactly 19 cubes? What are their dimensions?

6. How many different rectangular solids can you construct with exactly 36 cubes? What are their dimensions?

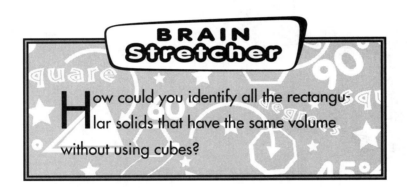

BRAIN Stretcher

How could you identify all the rectangular solids that have the same volume without using cubes?

⌇⌇VII⌇⌇

ODDS AND ENDS

You've learned a lot about geometry in a short time! There's even more to find out. This chapter presents just a taste of some other geometry concepts, such as graphing and symmetry. As you learn about these things, you'll have fun playing a shape comparison game, hunting for a target, and creating a mystery picture.

Shape Comparison

Play this game to practice finding and comparing the areas of various shapes.

MATERIALS

2 players
pencil
16 index cards
colored pencils
or crayons
ruler
paper

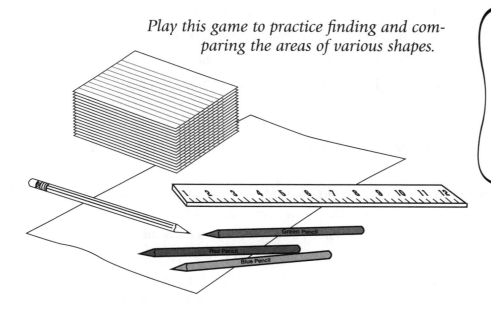

Game Preparation

1. Draw one of the following shapes on each of the index cards. Color in all of the shapes with colored pencils or crayons.

A square with sides that are 3 inches long

A square with sides that are 2 inches long

A right triangle with legs that are 3 and 5 inches long

A right triangle with legs that are 2 and 5 inches long

A rectangle with sides that are 1 and 4 inches long

A rectangle with sides that are 2 and 3 inches long

A rectangle with sides that are 3 and 5 inches long

A rectangle with sides that are 2 and 5 inches long

A rectangle with sides that are 1 and 5 inches long

A rectangle with sides that are 3 and 4 inches long

A circle with a radius of 3 inches

A circle with a radius of 2 inches

A parallelogram with a height of 2 inches and a length of 3 inches

A parallelogram with a height of 3 inches and a length of 4 inches

A parallelogram with a height of 1 inch and a length of 4 inches

A parallelogram with a height of 2 inches and a length of 4 inches

Game Rules

1. Players place all the cards facedown on the center of the table. Each player picks up one card.

2. Each player calculates the area of the figure on his or her card. The player with the card that has the smallest area wins both cards. If both cards have the same area, the cards are replaced and the players each pick a new card.

3. When there are no more cards on the table, the player with the most cards wins the game. If the game ends in a tie, the player who won the card with the smallest area wins the game.

Bull's Eye

Have you ever played Battleship? Plotting coordinate points on a graph is a lot like playing that game. In this activity, you will learn how to plot coordinate points and use them to play a game of Bull's Eye.

MATERIALS

2 players
2 sheets of
graph paper
2 pencils

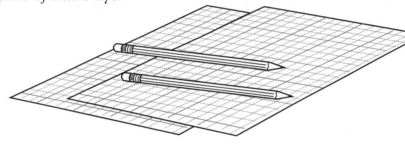

Game Preparation

1. Players first draw a straight horizontal line across the middle of the graph paper. Label the center point on the line 0. From the right of that point, label each point where a vertical line intersects your horizontal line 1, 2, 3, and so on, up to 10. To the left of the 0, label each point where a vertical line intersects your horizontal line −1, −2, −3, and so on, up to −10.

2. Players draw a vertical line across the paper that intersects the 0 point on the horizontal line at a right angle. Label the points above the horizontal line 1, 2, 3, and so on, up to 10. Label the points below the horizontal line −1, −2, −3, and so on, up to −10.

3. The two lines you made on the graph paper are called **coordinate axes**. The horizontal line is the *x*-axis, and the vertical line is the *y*-axis.

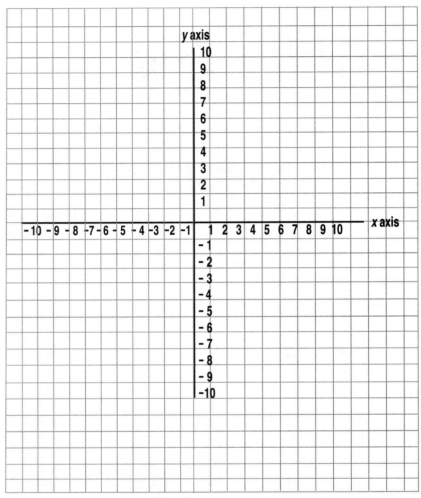

Coordinate axes

Game Rules

1. Players each draw a square with sides 5 boxes long on their coordinate axis. Players each draw a square with sides 3 boxes long inside the square with 5-box-long sides. Players shade the center box of their squares. Players should not let the other see the location of their bull's eye.

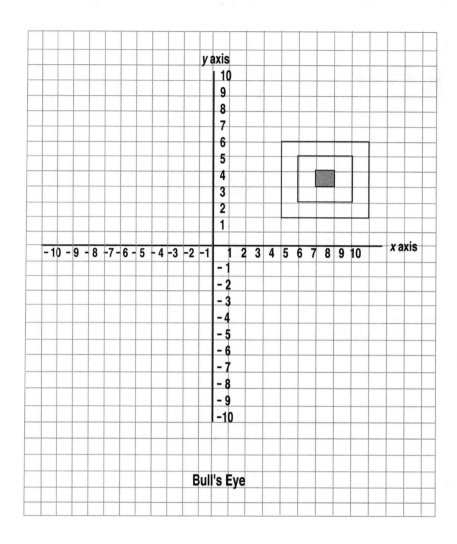

2. Players take turns calling out coordinate points, such as (3, 3), (–2, 1), etc., while the other player looks for that point on his or her graph. If a player's point lies on the outer square, the other player says, "warm." If a player's point lies on the inner square, the other player says, "hot." If a player's point lands on the small center square, the other player says, "bull's eye," and that player wins the game.

39

Mystery Picture

Find coordinate points to draw a mystery picture.

MATERIALS

pencil
graph paper

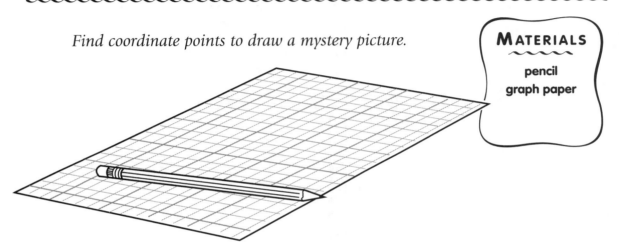

Procedure

1. Draw a set of coordinate axes on graph paper and graph the following points. Connect the points as you graph them.

(0, 0)	(0, 6)
(4, 4)	(−1, 7)
(4, 6)	(−3, 7)
(3, 7)	(−4, 6)
(1, 7)	(−4, 4)

What did you just draw using the connect-the-points method?

110

2. Graph and connect each of these pairs of points.

Connect (–3, 0) and (3, 0)

Connect (–3,0) and (2, –3)

Connect (–2, –3) and (3, 0)

Connect (0, 2) and (–2, –3)

Connect (0, 2) and (2, –3)

What did you just draw using the straight-line method?

BRAIN Stretchers

1. Write your name in block letters using coordinate points and the straight-line method.

2. Write your name in script using coordinate points and the connect-the-points method.

40

Number Symmetry

*Symmetry is the property of some geometrical shapes whose parts look like mirror images of one another when the shape is split in half. A **line of symmetry** is the line around which the shape is symmetrical. Symmetry can be horizontal, vertical, or both. Try this activity to find out if numerals are symmetrical.*

MATERIALS

paper
marker
small hand mirror
pencil

Procedure

1. Use the marker to write the numerals from 0 to 9 on paper. Make the numerals about 2 inches tall.

2. Place the mirror vertically down the center of the zero so that you can see the other half of the zero in the mirror. You are conducting a vertical symmetry test. Look in the mirror. Is a complete zero formed by the combination of the half zero on the paper and the half zero in the reflection? If it is, then a zero has vertical symmetry. Enter the word *yes* in a chart like the one on page 113.

3. Place the mirror horizontally across the center of the zero to conduct a horizontal symmetry test. Look in the mirror. Is a zero formed in the reflection? If it is, then a zero has horizontal symmetry. Enter the word *yes* in your chart.

4. Perform both the horizontal and the vertical symmetry test on each numeral from 1 to 9. Enter the results in your chart.

Numeral	Vertical Symmetry	Horizontal Symmetry
0		
1		
2		
3		
4		
5		
6		
7		
8		
9		

5. Which numerals have horizontal symmetry?

6. Which numerals have vertical symmetry?

7. Which numerals have both vertical and horizontal symmetry?

1. Draw all the capital letters from A to Z on a sheet of paper. Use a mirror to test the vertical and horizontal symmetry of these letters. Draw a chart and enter the results in the chart.

2. Test the lowercase letters for horizontal and vertical symmetry.

3. Some symmetrical figures have more than two lines of symmetry. Draw some different shapes, such as triangles and snowflakes, and cut them out. Fold the paper in as many ways as you can to get mirror images. What shape has the most lines of symmetry?

GEOMETRY MASTER CERTIFICATE

Now that you've mastered all the geometry facts, problems, and games in this book, you are officially certified as a geometry master! Make a photocopy of this certificate, write your name on the copy, and hang it on the wall.

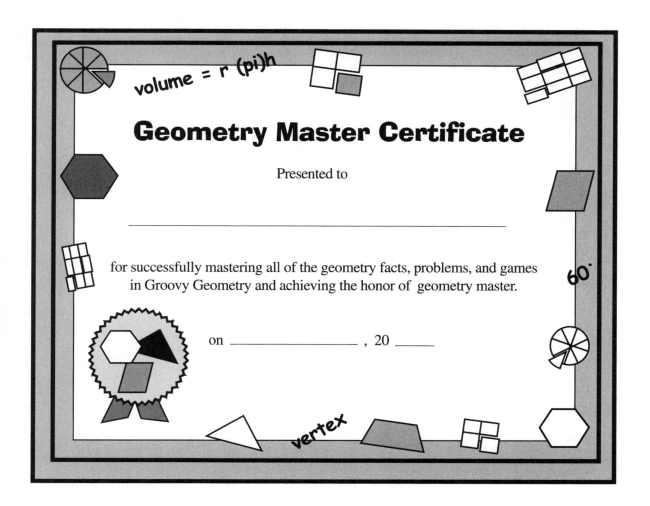

volume = r (pi)h

Geometry Master Certificate

Presented to

_____

for successfully mastering all of the geometry facts, problems, and games in Groovy Geometry and achieving the honor of geometry master.

60°

on _____ , 20 _____

vertex

Index

acute angles, 3, 4
acute triangles, 25–26
alternate angles, 15–17
angles
  acute, 3, 4
  alternate, 15–17
  complementary, supplementary, and
    vertical, 13–14, 17
  corresponding, 16–17
  definition of, 3
  drawing, 8–10
  exterior, 15–17, 31–34
  identifying, 4
  interior, 15–17, 34
  measuring, 5–7
  naming, 11–12
  obtuse, 3, 4
  of circles, 86–87
  of quadrilaterals, 58–60
  pairs of, 13–14
  parallel lines, transversal, and, 15–17
  right, 3, 4, 18, 20–21
area
  definition of, 35
  of circle, 81–82, 83–85
  of parallelogram, 66–67
  of rectangle, 35, 64–65
  of shapes, comparing, 105–106
  of square, 62–63
  of triangle, 35–38
  See also surface area
axes, coordinate, 107

calculating
  area of circle, 83–85
  circumference with pi, 80
  measures of angles, 13–14
  volume of cube, 97–98

volume of cylinder, 99–100
  See also measuring
circles
  area of, 81–82, 83–85
  central angles of, 86–87
  creating perfect, 75–76
  parts of, 73
  pi and, 77–79
circumference
  definition of, 75
  finding, 77–79, 80
complementary angles,
  13–14
computing. *See* calculating
cones
  creating, 91–93
  definition of, 90
congruent triangles, 39–41
coordinate axes, 107
coordinate points
  drawing picture with,
    110–111
  plotting on graph, 107–109
corresponding angles, 16–17
cubes
  creating, 91–93
  definition of, 90
  volume of, 97–98
cylinders
  creating, 91–93
  definition of, 90
  surface area of, 95–96
  volume of, 99–100

decagons, 71–72
diameter
  definition of, 75
  measuring, 77–79

drawing
  angles, 8–10
  picture with coordinate points, 110–111

edge, 89
equilateral triangles, 25–26
exterior angles
  measuring, 15–17
  of triangle, 31–34

face, 89
formulas
  area of circle, 83–85
  area of triangle, 38

games
  Angle Pairs, 13–14
  Bull's Eye, 107–109
  Crazy about Quadrilaterals, 55–57
  Draw It!, 8–10
  Name Game, 11–12
  Rectangle Race, 64–65
  Right-Angle Scavenger Hunt, 20–21
  Shape Comparison, 105–106
  Triangle Memory, 27–28
geometry
  definition of, 1
  learning, 2
Geometry Master Certificate, 115
graphs
  drawing picture with coordinate points,
    110–111
  plotting coordinate points on, 107–109

heptagons, 23, 71–72
hexagons, 23, 71–72
horizontal symmetry, 112–114
hypotenuse, 45

interior angles
  measuring, 15–17

remote, 34
isosceles triangles, 25–26

kites, 55–57

legs, 45
line of symmetry, 112–114
line segments, 2
lines
  definition of, 2
  perpendicular, 18–19

measuring
  angles, 5–7
  area of triangle, 35–38
  diameter, 77–79
  exterior angles, 15–17, 31–34
  perimeter of quadrilateral, 61
  surface area, 94, 95–96
  See also calculating

naming angles, 11–12
nonagons, 71–72

obtuse angles, 3, 4
obtuse triangles, 25–26
octagons, 71–72
origin, 75

parallel lines, 15
parallelograms
  changing into rectangles,
    66–67
  definition of, 55
  matching, 55–57
pentagons
  angles of, 60
  creating, 71–72
  definition of, 23
perfect squares, 45–48
perimeter, 61

perpendicular lines, 18–19
pi
  calculating circumference with, 80
  finding, 77–79
plane geometry, 2
planes, 2
points
  definition of, 2
  plotting on graph, 107–109,
    110–111
polygons
  definition of, 23–24
  types of, 71–72
  See also triangles
polyhedrons, 89–90
prisms, 90
proportion, 42
protractor, using, 5–7
pyramids
  creating, 91–93
  definition of, 90
Pythagorean theorem
  perfect squares, 45–48
  proving, 49–51

quadrilaterals
  angles of, 58–60
  definition of, 53
  perimeter of, 61
  types of, 55–57
  See also rectangles; squares

radius, 75
rays, 2, 3
rectangles
  area of, 35, 64–65
  changing parallelograms into,
    66–67
  definition of, 55–57
rectangular solids
  creating, 91–93

surface area of, 94
  volume of, 101–102
remote interior angles, 34
rhombuses
  definition of, 55
  making patterns with, 68–70
  matching, 55–57
right angles
  definition of, 3, 4
  finding, 20–21
  perpendicular lines and, 18
right triangles, 25–26

scalene triangles, 25–26
shapes, comparing area of,
    105–106
similar triangles, 42–44
solid geometry, 2
solids
  creating, 91–93
  types of, 89–90
  See also surface area
spheres
  creating, 91–93
  definition of, 90
squares
  area of, 62–63
  definition of, 55–57
  perfect, 45–48
  rhombuses compared to, 68
squaring, 45
supplementary angles, 13–14, 17
surface area
  cylinder, 95–96
  rectangular solid, 94
symmetry, 112–114

transversals, 15
trapezoids
  making patterns with, 68–70
  matching, 55–57

triangles
  acute, 25–26
  area of, 35–38
  congruent, 39–41
  equilateral, 25–26
  exterior angles of, 31–34
  hypotenuse of, 45
  isosceles, 25–26
  matching, 27–28
  obtuse, 25–26
  Pythagorean theorem and, 45–48
  right, 25–26
  scalene, 25–26
  similar, 42–44
  sum of angles of, 29–30
  types of, 24, 25–26

vertex/vertices
  of angle, 3
  of parallelogram, 66
  of solid, 89
vertical angles, 13–14
vertical symmetry, 112–114
volume
  of cube, 97–98
  of cylinder, 99–100
  of rectangular solid, 101–102

x-axis, 107

y-axis, 107

Children/Mathematics $14.95 USA / $17.99 CAN

Don't Just Learn Geometry. . . Master It!

Brimming with fun and educational games and activities, the Magical Math series provides everything you need to know to become a master of mathematics! In each of these books, Lynette Long uses her unique style to help you truly understand mathematical concepts as you use common objects such as playing cards, dice, coins, and every mathematician's basic tools: paper and pencil.

Inside *Groovy Geometry,* you'll find all the geometry basics, plus information on how to figure out the height of any object from its shadow, find distances "as the crow flies," estimate the area of any space, and much more. While you play the Name Game and Rectangle Race, you'll learn how to draw, measure, and identify different kinds of angles, triangles, and quadrilaterals. And with fun activities like Bull's Eye and Pizza Party, you'll practice plotting coordinate points on a graph and measuring the area and diameter of a circle. Most important, you'll have a great time doing it!

So why wait? Jump right in and find out how easy it is to become a mathematics master!

LYNETTE LONG, PH.D., is the author of several children's math books, including *Fabulous Fractions, Measurement Mania, Dazzling Division, Marvelous Multiplication,* and *Delightful Decimals and Perfect Percents,* all from Wiley. She has taught math and was a professor of education, specializing in mathematics education.

Cover Design: José Almaguer
Cover Illustration: © Doug Jones

www.josseybass.com

JOSSEY-BASS™
An Imprint of
WILEY

ISBN 978-0-471-21059-7